THE WORLD ALMANAC

AWESOME TRUE -OR- FALSE QUESTIONS FOR SMART KIDS

-ANIMALS-

THE WORLD ALMANAC™

AWESOME TRUE -OR- FALSE QUESTIONS FOR SMART KIDS -ANIMALS-

WORLD ALMANAC BOOKS

World Almanac books may be purchased in bulk at special discounts for sales promotion, corporate gifts, fund-raising, or educational purposes. Special editions can also be created to specifications. For details, contact the Special Sales Department, Skyhorse Publishing, 307 West 36th Street, 11th Floor, New York, NY 10018 or info@skyhorsepublishing.com.

Published by World Almanac, an imprint of Skyhorse Publishing, Inc.
307 West 36th Street, 11th Floor, New York, NY 10018.

www.skyhorsepublishing.com

10 9 8 7 6 5 4 3 2 1

Cover design by Kai Texel
Illustrations by Alex Paterson
Page composition/typography by Joshua Barnaby

Library of Congress Cataloging-in-Publication Data is available on file.

Print ISBN: 978-1-5107-6747-8
Ebook ISBN: 978-1-5107-6748-5

Printed in the United States of America

THE WORLD ALMANAC AWESOME TRUE-OR-FALSE QUESTIONS FOR SMART KIDS: ANIMALS

USER'S NOTE

On the front side of every page, you will find true-or-false statements. Some answers might be easy and others will not! Give each one your best guess, or use them to challenge a friend.

Then turn the page. You will find the correct answers right there, on the back side of each page.

The next page will have even more fun true-or-false tidbits to keep you guessing until the very end!

THE WORLD ALMANAC™

AWESOME TRUE -or- FALSE QUESTIONS FOR SMART KIDS

-ANIMALS-

1. COWS HAVE FOUR STOMACHS.

TRUE OR FALSE?

2. CATS SAY A FRIENDLY HELLO BY HISSING.

TRUE OR FALSE?

3. COWS HAVE BEST FRIENDS AND LIKE TO HANG OUT TOGETHER.

TRUE OR FALSE?

4. BUTTERFLIES TASTE WITH THEIR FEET.

TRUE OR FALSE?

See the back of the page to find out.

1. **False.** Cows have one stomach with four compartments: the rumen; reticulum; omasum; and abomasum.

2. **False.** Hissing is a distance-increasing behavior. Cats sometimes say hello by pressing their noses together.

3. **True.** According to research by Krista McLennan at University of Northampton, cows showed signs of stress and agitation, such as higher heart rates, when separated from their preferred companions.

4. **True.** Butterflies use taste sensors on their feet to locate food for their caterpillars. If they find a plant with food for their caterpillars, they lay their eggs there.

5. DOLPHINS HAVE NAMES FOR EACH OTHER.

TRUE OR FALSE?

6. THERE ARE ONLY TWO KNOWN SPECIES OF KANGAROOS.

TRUE OR FALSE?

7. POLAR BEARS ARE LEFT-HANDED.

TRUE OR FALSE?

See the back of the page to find out.

5. **True.** Dolphins use a unique whistle to identify each other.

6. **False.** There are at least 40 known species of kangaroo. A male kangaroo is known as a boomer, a female kangaroo is a flyer, and a baby kangaroo a joey.

7. **False.** It was once commonly thought that polar bears were left-handed but scientists who study polar bears have found no evidence of this.

8. MALE PUPPIES ALWAYS WIN WHEN THEY PLAY WITH FEMALE PUPPIES BECAUSE THEY TEND TO BE BIGGER.

TRUE OR FALSE?

9. FEMALE BATS GIVE BIRTH IN A NEST.

TRUE OR FALSE?

10. HOUSEFLIES ALL BUZZ IN THE SAME MUSICAL KEY.

TRUE OR FALSE?

11. FENNEC FOXES HAVE SUPER FURRY FEET TO KEEP THEIR FEET WARM.

TRUE OR FALSE?

12. TOUCANS CURL INTO BALLS WHEN THEY SLEEP.

TRUE OR FALSE?

See the back of the page to find out.

8. **False.** Male puppies often let female puppies win, even when the male puppies are larger or stronger.

9. **False.** Female bats give birth upside down and catch the baby bat in their wings.

10. **True.** The human ear interprets the noise made by a housefly flapping its wings as a pitch along the F major scale. The common housefly flaps its wings about 190 times per second.

11. **False.** Fennec foxes have furry feet to protect their feet from the hot desert sand in their native habitat.

12. **True.** When they sleep, toucans turn their head so that their long, often-colorful bill rests on their back and their tail is folded over their head.

13. KANGAROOS CAN'T FART.

TRUE OR FALSE?

14. CENTIPEDES ALWAYS HAVE 100 LEGS.

TRUE OR FALSE?

15. A MILLIPEDE HAS AT LEAST 1,000 LEGS.

TRUE OR FALSE?

16. SPIDERS ALWAYS HAVE EIGHT LEGS.

TRUE OR FALSE?

17. A SHARK CAN HAVE UP TO 35,000 TEETH IN ITS LIFETIME.

TRUE OR FALSE?

See the back of the page to find out.

13. **False.** Scientists in the 1970s and 1980s believed this to be true, but more recent studies show kangaroos fart as much as other animals their size.

14. **False.** Even though "centipede" means "100 feet," the number of legs on an individual centipede depends on its number of body segments. Centipedes range from 15 to 177 pairs of legs.

15. **False.** Millipedes generally have between 24 and 750 legs.

16. **True.** Spiders have eight legs that they walk on. Spiders also have pedipalps, a pair of appendages that they use like arms.

17. **True.** Carcharhiniformes, the largest order of sharks, constantly shed their teeth and grow new ones.

18. MOST SHARKS HAVE FIVE ROWS OF TEETH.

TRUE OR FALSE?

19. SHARKS' UPPER AND LOWER JAWS BOTH MOVE.

TRUE OR FALSE?

20. ELEPHANTS CAN LIVE TO BE 80 YEARS OLD.

TRUE OR FALSE?

21. AN OSTRICH'S EYE IS BIGGER THAN ITS BRAIN.

TRUE OR FALSE?

22. GIRAFFES CLEAN THEIR EYES AND EARS WITH THEIR TONGUES.

TRUE OR FALSE?

23. OSTRICHES BURY THEIR HEADS IN THE SAND WHEN THEY ARE SCARED.

TRUE OR FALSE?

See the back of the page to find out.

18. **True.** Sharks can have up to 15 rows of teeth but most have five.

19. **True.** Most animals move only their lower jaw but sharks can move both.

20. **True.** Elephants, whales, and humans are among the longest living mammals with life expectancies ranging from 70 to 100+ years.

21. **True.** An ostrich eye is about the size of a billiard ball and its brain is smaller.

22. **True.** Giraffe tongues can be 18-20 inches long and are used for grooming.

23. **False.** Ostriches have very small heads and it only looks as though they are burying them. Ostriches frequently lay eggs in nests dug into the ground and use their heads to turn the eggs several times a day.

24. BIRDS WILL ABANDON THEIR NESTS AND OFFSPRING IF THEY CAN SMELL THAT A PERSON HAS TOUCHED THEM.

TRUE OR FALSE?

25. AFTER A FEMALE PENGUIN LAYS AN EGG, THE MALE PENGUIN IS RESPONSIBLE FOR GETTING IT TO HATCH.

TRUE OR FALSE?

26. THE LARGEST FISH IS THE BLUE WHALE.

TRUE OR FALSE?

27. A WHALE SHARK CAN BE UP TO 60 FEET LONG.

TRUE OR FALSE?

28. A SHARK CAN BE A VEGETARIAN.

TRUE OR FALSE?

24. **False.** Birds have a poorly developed sense of smell and can't detect a human scent.

25. **True.** Male penguins balance the egg on their feet and keep it warm surrounded by feathered skin known as a brood pouch.

26. **False.** A blue whale can weigh up to 400,000 pounds—the weight of 33 elephants—but it is a mammal, not a fish.

27. **True.** The whale shark is the largest known living species of fish.

28. **False.** Most sharks are carnivores, or meat eaters. The bonnethead shark, one of the smaller hammerhead sharks, eats sea grasses along with crustaceans and mollusks. This means the bonnethead is an omnivore but not a vegetarian.

29. SLOTHS CAN'T SWIM.

TRUE OR FALSE?

30. SLOTHS ONLY POOP ONCE A WEEK.

TRUE OR FALSE?

31. SLOTHS CAN HOLD THEIR BREATH FOR MORE THAN HALF AN HOUR.

TRUE OR FALSE?

See the back of the page to find out.

29. **False.** Sloths swim three times faster than they can move on land.

 30. **True.** Sloth digestion moves slowly and they only defecate about every five to seven days.

31. **True.** Sloths can stay underwater for up to 40 minutes.

32. ZEBRAS HAVE STRIPES FOR CAMOUFLAGE.

TRUE OR FALSE?

33. ZEBRAS' STRIPE PATTERNS ARE AS UNIQUE AS FINGERPRINTS.

TRUE OR FALSE?

34. GIRAFFE SKIN IS LIGHT TAN.

TRUE OR FALSE?

35. POLAR BEARS HAVE BLACK SKIN.

TRUE OR FALSE?

36. POLAR BEARS LIVE AT THE SOUTH POLE.

TRUE OR FALSE?

37. A JELLYFISH CAN BE LARGER THAN A PERSON.

TRUE OR FALSE?

See the back of the page to find out.

32. **False.** Scientists now think that zebra stripes exist to help ward off flies that can carry deadly diseases and/or to help regulate their body temperature.

33. **True.** Zebra stripes are unique to each individual animal. Some researchers have used zebras' individual stripe patterns to identify and track them.

34. **True.** Giraffe skin is all one color but their coats are multicolored.

35. **True.** The skin under polar bears' fur is black to absorb sunshine and help warm them.

36. **False.** Polar bears only live in the northern hemisphere.

37. **True.** The Lion's Mane jellyfish can be almost 6 feet wide with tentacles almost 50 feet long.

38. SHRIMP CAN SMELL THINGS.

   TRUE OR FALSE?   ← ← ← ←

39. SNAKES SHED THEIR SKIN.

   TRUE OR FALSE?

40. BEARS SLEEP ALL WINTER.

   TRUE OR FALSE?

41. DURING THE FALL, BEARS CAN GAIN UP TO THREE POUNDS A DAY.

   TRUE OR FALSE?

What?

See the back of the page to find out.

← *38.* **True.** Shrimp have antennae with sensors that allow them to taste or smell by sampling chemicals in the water.

39. **True.** Snakes shed their skin when they grow or when the skin is old and worn. There is a new layer of skin underneath.

40. **False.** Bears hibernate, which means they don't need to eat or drink, but they wake up and move around their den.

41. **True.** Bears can spend up to 20 hours a day foraging in order to gain weight to prepare for hibernation.

42. THE FIRST ANIMAL IN SPACE WAS A MONKEY.

TRUE OR FALSE?

43. FEMALE LOBSTERS LAY EGGS.

TRUE OR FALSE?

44. LOBSTER SHELLS GROW AS A LOBSTER GETS BIGGER.

TRUE OR FALSE?

45. LIVE LOBSTERS ARE RED.

TRUE OR FALSE?

46. LOBSTERS CAN GROW NEW LEGS.

TRUE OR FALSE?

42. **False.** Albert II was the first monkey in space on June 4, 1949, but a group of fruit flies had been launched into space on February 20, 1947.

43. **True.** The female lobster carries eggs inside for as many as 9 to 12 months and then attached under her tail for another 10 to 11 months.

44. **False.** Lobsters molt, or shed their shells, about 25 times in the first five to seven years of their lives.

45. **False.** Lobsters are typically blue-green or green-brown while they are alive but turn red when they are cooked.

46. **True.** Lobsters can discard a leg when in trouble (this is called reflex amputation) and grow a new one.

47. Lobsters have teeth.

TRUE OR FALSE?

48. A fish can be 100 years old.

TRUE OR FALSE?

49. Sharks have eyelids.

TRUE OR FALSE?

50. Sharks don't have bones.

TRUE OR FALSE?

51. Sharks have poor vision.

TRUE OR FALSE?

52. Sharks have eight senses.

TRUE OR FALSE?

53. Sharks are always hungry.

TRUE OR FALSE?

See the back of the page to find out.

47. **True.** Lobsters' teeth are in their stomachs and are called the gastric mill.

48. **True.** Several different species of fish have been known to live 100 years.

49. **True.** Most fish do not have eyelids but sharks do.

50. **True.** Technically, sharks have cartilage.

51. **False.** Sharks have extremely good vision and see well even in dim light.

52. **True.** Sharks' eight senses are hearing, smell, touch, taste, sight, pressure changes/lateral line, pit organs, and electroreception (called the ampullae of Lorenzini).

53. **False.** Sharks can go up to six weeks without feeding. One Swell Shark was observed not eating for 15 months.

54. A FULL SUIT OF ARMOR WAS ONCE FOUND IN THE BELLY OF A SHARK.

TRUE OR FALSE?

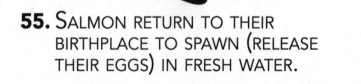

55. SALMON RETURN TO THEIR BIRTHPLACE TO SPAWN (RELEASE THEIR EGGS) IN FRESH WATER.

TRUE OR FALSE?

54. **True.** Some sharks will eat almost anything. Some of the odder items found inside sharks include tires, license plates, a fur coat, and even a whole chicken coop.

55. **True.** Salmon usually return to the river system and sometimes the very stream where they were born, even though they spend most of their lives in ocean salt water.

56. A SHRIMP CAN GROW UP TO A FOOT LONG.

TRUE OR FALSE?

57. SEALS DON'T DRINK WATER.

TRUE OR FALSE?

58. SEALS NEED TO STAY WET.

TRUE OR FALSE?

59. DUCKS CAN SLEEP WITH ONE EYE OPEN.

TRUE OR FALSE?

60. MOST HUMMINGBIRDS WEIGH LESS THAN A NICKEL.

TRUE OR FALSE?

61. A PARROT CAN ONLY LEARN UP TO 50 WORDS.

TRUE OR FALSE?

See the back of the page to find out.

56. **True.** Shrimp species vary in size when fully grown from a few millimeters to over 12 inches.

57. **True.** Like most marine animals, seals' bodies are efficient at removing water from their food.

58. **False.** Seals don't need to be wet constantly. They come out of water to dry off.

59. **True.** While most ducks in a flock sleep more deeply, those on lookout keep one eye open to be aware of predators.

60. **True.** The average hummingbird weighs around four grams, one gram less than a nickel.

61. **False.** Einstein, an African grey parrot at a Knoxville, Tennessee, zoo knew at least 200 words.

62. AARDVARKS ARE NATIVELY FOUND IN FLORIDA.

TRUE OR FALSE?

63. NEWFOUNDLAND DOGS HAVE WEBBED FEET.

TRUE OR FALSE?

64. A DOG'S NOSE PRINT IS UNIQUE.

TRUE OR FALSE?

See the back of the page to find out.

62. **False.** Aardvarks are nocturnal burrowing creatures that are native to Africa. The name "aardvark" means "earth pig" in South Africa's Afrikaans language.

63. **True.** Newfoundlands' webbed feet and waterproof coats make them excellent swimmers.

64. **True.** A dog's nose print is unique and can be used for identification, much like a human's fingerprint.

65. DOGS CANNOT GIVE BIRTH TO MORE THAN 10 PUPPIES IN A SINGLE LITTER.

TRUE OR FALSE?

66. A DOG'S NOSE CAN BE MORE THAN 50 TIMES AS SENSITIVE AS A HUMAN NOSE.

TRUE OR FALSE?

67. DOGS CAN BE TRAINED TO DETECT TRUFFLES, THE VALUABLE FUNGUS THAT GROWS UNDERGROUND.

TRUE OR FALSE?

68. GREYHOUND DOGS ARE FASTER THAN CHEETAHS IN A LONG RACE.

TRUE OR FALSE?

69. DOGS HAVE EXCELLENT NIGHT VISION.

TRUE OR FALSE?

65. **False.** According to Guinness World Records, the largest dog litter ever was 24 Neapolitan mastiff puppies born in one litter in 2004.

66. **True.** While a human nose has about 5 million scent receptors, a dog's nose can have as many as 300 million scent receptors.

 67. **True.** Traditionally, truffle hunters used pigs to find truffles, but pigs were known to sometimes eat what they found. Dogs trained to hunt truffles do not eat them.

68. **True.** In short distances a cheetah is much faster than a greyhound but can only maintain its top speed for several hundred yards. A greyhound can run 35 miles per hour for up to 7 miles.

69. **True.** Dogs have a part of their eyes called the *tapetum lucidum* that helps them see at night.

70. THE DOG BREED "COLLIE" MEANS "SHEEP."

TRUE OR FALSE?

71. A DOG IS AS SMART AS A TWO-YEAR-OLD CHILD.

TRUE OR FALSE?

72. THE BASENJI DOG DOESN'T MAKE ANY SOUNDS.

TRUE OR FALSE?

73. DOGS NEVER SWEAT.

TRUE OR FALSE?

74. THE DOG BREED SHIH TZU MEANS "LITTLE LION."

TRUE OR FALSE?

70. **False.** Collie is believed to be from "Coll," the Anglo-Saxon word for "black."

71. **True.** Dogs and two-year-old children are both capable of understanding up to 250 words and gestures.

72. **False.** The Basenji breed doesn't bark but they do make a sound that is compared to yodeling.

73. **False.** While dogs mostly pant, instead of sweat, to cool themselves, their paw pads can sweat.

74. **True.** Shih Tzu translates to "little lion" in Mandarin Chinese.

75. THE AUSTRALIAN SHEPHERD IS AN AMERICAN BREED OF DOG.

TRUE OR FALSE?

76. DOGS ALL HAVE PINK TONGUES.

TRUE OR FALSE?

77. DOGS CAN DETECT THE EARTH'S MAGNETIC FIELD.

TRUE OR FALSE?

78. WHEN A DOG WAGS ITS TAIL IT ALWAYS MEANS IT IS HAPPY.

TRUE OR FALSE?

79. DOGS ONLY YAWN WHEN THEY ARE TIRED.

TRUE OR FALSE?

See the back of the page to find out.

75. **True.** The Australian Shepherd is not from Australia.

76. **False.** The dog breeds Chow Chow and Shar-Pei have blue-black tongues, as do some other mixed breeds. Some dogs have tongues with black spots.

77. **True.** Czech scientists in 2014 found evidence that when dogs circle to go to the bathroom, they tend to align themselves on a North-South axis.

78. **False.** Dogs use different tail positions and wags to show their state of mind. Studies show that dogs wag their tails to the right when they are happy and to the left when they are frightened.

79. **False.** While dogs can yawn when they are tired, repeated yawns can signify that a dog is feeling anxious or stressed.

80. CHOCOLATE CAN BE DANGEROUS TO DOGS.

TRUE OR FALSE?

81. ALL DOGS CAN SWIM.

TRUE OR FALSE?

82. THE LABRADOR RETRIEVER IS THE MOST POPULAR DOG BREED IN THE UNITED STATES.

TRUE OR FALSE?

83. WHEN PETTING A DOG, HUMAN BLOOD PRESSURE GOES DOWN.

TRUE OR FALSE?

84. DOGS SNIFF BUTTS TO LEARN ABOUT EACH OTHER.

TRUE OR FALSE?

80. **True.** Theobromine, a naturally occurring chemical compound found in chocolate, can build up in dogs and become deadly.

81. **False.** Many dogs can't swim due to their anatomic or facial structure. Basset hounds, bulldogs, dachshunds, and pugs are all unlikely to be swimmers.

82. **True.** The Labrador retriever has been number-one on the American Kennel Club's list of dog breeds since 1991.

83. **True.** When a person pets a dog, both the person and the dog experience a lowering of their blood pressure.

84. **True.** A dog's unique smell is secreted from scent-producing glands that are located in their backsides.

85. PUPPIES ARE BORN DEAF.

    TRUE OR FALSE?

86. DOGS SEE EVERYTHING IN BLACK AND WHITE.

    TRUE OR FALSE?

87. DALMATIAN PUPPIES ARE BORN WITH SPOTS.

    TRUE OR FALSE?

88. HUMANS HAVE MORE TASTE BUDS THAN DOGS.

    TRUE OR FALSE?

89. ONE DOG YEAR IS ALWAYS EQUAL TO SEVEN HUMAN YEARS.

    TRUE OR FALSE?

85. **True.** Puppies do not develop the ability to hear until they are about three weeks old. When they are grown, they can hear four times better than humans.

86. **False.** While dogs don't see all colors, they do see blue and yellow.

87. **False.** Dalmatians are born completely white and develop spots as they grow older, usually by the age of three or four months.

88. **True.** Dogs have about 1,700 taste buds while humans have up to 10,000 taste buds.

89. **False.** While the average medium size dog lives about one-seventh of the typical human's life expectancy, the first year of a dog's life is equal in development to about 15 human years.

90. Dog noses are wet to keep them cool.

TRUE OR FALSE? ← ← ← ←

91. Dogs have three eyelids.

TRUE OR FALSE?

92. Onions are toxic to dogs.

TRUE OR FALSE?

93. Cats spend up to 70 percent of their lives sleeping.

TRUE OR FALSE?

94. Most cats have 20 toes.

TRUE OR FALSE?

95. Cats walk like camels and giraffes.

TRUE OR FALSE?

← 90. **False.** Dog noses are wet to help them absorb scent chemicals. They lick their noses to help them identify smells.

🐾 91. **True.** They have what is called a nictitating membrane that helps remove dust and mucus from their eyes.

🐾 92. **True.** Onions, garlic, and other alliums can cause anemia in dogs.

🐾 93. **True.** Cats generally sleep an average of 13 to 16 hours a day but sometimes sleep 20 hours during a 24-hour period.

🐾 94. **False.** Most cats have 18 toes; five on each front paw and four on each back paw.

🐾 95. **True.** They move both right feet at the same time and both left feet at the same time.

96. CATS ARE VERY CLEAN.

TRUE OR FALSE?

97. A CAT WITH A QUESTION MARK-SHAPED TAIL IS ANGRY.

TRUE OR FALSE?

98. CATS CAN JUMP UP TO SIX TIMES THEIR LENGTH.

TRUE OR FALSE?

See the back of the page to find out.

96. **True.** They spend up to a third of their waking hours grooming themselves.

97. **False.** A question mark-shaped tail typically means a cat wants to play.

98. **True.** An active, average-sized cat can jump some eight feet in a single leap.

99. CATS CAN'T CLIMB DOWN A TREE.

TRUE OR FALSE?

100. CATS HAVE FEWER BONES THAN A HUMAN.

TRUE OR FALSE?

101. PRESIDENT ABRAHAM LINCOLN LOVED CATS.

TRUE OR FALSE?

See the back of the page to find out.

99. **True.** Their retractable claws curve in a way that makes climbing down trees nearly impossible compared to climbing up.

100. **False.** Cats have 230 bones. Humans have 206.

101. **True.** President Lincoln had several cats while living in the White House and is said to have once observed that one of his cats was "smarter than my whole cabinet."

102. A GROUP OF KITTENS IS CALLED A PACK.

TRUE OR FALSE?

103. CATS HAVE SMALL EYES.

TRUE OR FALSE?

104. CATS HAVE ROUGH TONGUES.

TRUE OR FALSE?

105. CATS CAN BE RIGHT- OR LEFT-PAWED (IN THE SAME WAY THAT HUMANS ARE RIGHT- OR LEFT-HANDED).

TRUE OR FALSE?

106. CATS SOMETIMES GROOM OTHER CATS.

TRUE OR FALSE?

107. KITTENS IN THE SAME LITTER CAN HAVE MORE THAN ONE FATHER.

TRUE OR FALSE?

See the back of the page to find out.

102. **False.** A group of kittens is called a kindle.

103. **False.** They have the largest eyes relative to head size of any mammal.

104. **True.** Cat tongues are covered with tiny barbs that are helpful in grooming and can lick a bone clean of meat.

105. **True.** Studies have shown that many cats show "handedness." Furthermore female cats are likelier to be right-pawed and male cats are likelier to be left-pawed.

106. **True.** Cats grooming other cats is a behavior called allogrooming.

107. **True.** Female cats release eggs over several days when they are in heat.

108. HOUSE CATS CAN REACH SPEEDS OF 40 MILES PER HOUR.

TRUE OR FALSE?

109. CATS CANNOT BE VEGETARIANS.

TRUE OR FALSE?

110. CATS TWITCH THEIR TAILS FROM SIDE TO SIDE WHEN THEY ARE HAPPY.

TRUE OR FALSE?

111. CATS LOVE CANDY.

TRUE OR FALSE?

108. **False.** Cats can run very fast, though, up to 30 miles per hour.

109. **True.** Cats are "obligate carnivores," meaning they need certain nutrients that only come from eating meat or using nutritional supplements.

110. **False.** A cat typically twitches its tail like this to show that they are annoyed.

111. **False.** Cats are believed to be the only mammal that can't taste sweetness.

112. ADULT CATS MEOW TO TALK TO EACH OTHER.

TRUE OR FALSE?

113. ALL CATS LOVE MILK.

TRUE OR FALSE?

114. THERE ARE MORE REGISTERED BREEDS OF CATS THAN DOGS.

TRUE OR FALSE?

115. CATS MOVE THEIR JAWS LIKE HUMANS.

TRUE OR FALSE?

116. CATS HAVE 32 MUSCLES IN THEIR EARS.

TRUE OR FALSE?

117. CATS' HEARTS BEAT VERY FAST.

TRUE OR FALSE?

See the back of the page to find out.

112. **False.** They only meow to talk to humans.

113. **False.** Many cats are allergic to milk.

114. **False.** There are about 70 recognized cat breeds and more than 300 dog breeds, though different breed organizations' numbers vary widely.

115. **False.** Cats can only move their jaws up and down, not side to side.

116. **True.** The number of muscles in cats' ears enables them to rotate their ears widely to better receive sounds.

117. **True.** A cat's resting heart rate can be more than double that of a human.

118. THERE ARE MORE CATS THAN PEOPLE IN THE UNITED STATES.

TRUE OR FALSE?

119. CATS ARE MOST ACTIVE AT DAWN AND DUSK.

TRUE OR FALSE?

120. IT TAKES TWO WEEKS FROM BIRTH FOR A HORSE TO RUN.

TRUE OR FALSE?

121. HORSES DO NOT SEE COLORS.

TRUE OR FALSE?

122. FEMALE HORSES TYPICALLY HAVE FEWER TEETH THAN MALE HORSES.

TRUE OR FALSE?

118. **False.** More than 300 million people live in the United States and the cat population (including both house pets and feral cats) is probably around one-third of that.

119. **True.** Cats and dogs both exhibit what is called crepuscular behavior, or being most active at dawn and dusk.

120. **False.** A horse can run within hours of birth.

121. **False.** Horses can see differences between colors but they do not see the full spectrum in the same way as people.

122. **True.** Male horses have 40 teeth while female horses have 36.

123. At some point in a gallop all of a horses legs are off of the ground.

TRUE OR FALSE?

124. Horses only sleep lying down.

TRUE OR FALSE?

125. Horses can see almost 360 degrees completely around.

TRUE OR FALSE?

See the back of the page to find out.

123. **True.** The point in a horse's stride when all legs leave the ground was first visually documented in the 1870s by the stop action photography of Eadweard Muybridge.

124. **False.** Horses can sleep both lying down and standing up.

125. **True.** Horses have an extremely wide field of vision because their eyes are positioned on either side of their heads.

126. A HORSE'S BRAIN IS SMALLER THAN A HUMAN BRAIN.

TRUE OR FALSE?

127. HORSES LIKE SWEETS.

TRUE OR FALSE?

128. HORSE HEARTS ARE BIGGER THAN HUMAN HEARTS.

TRUE OR FALSE?

129. HORSES CAN'T GET SUNBURNED.

TRUE OR FALSE?

130. YOU CAN TELL IF A HORSE IS COLD BY FEELING HIS EARS.

TRUE OR FALSE?

131. HORSES DON'T DRINK A LOT.

TRUE OR FALSE?

See the back of the page to find out.

126. **True.** A fully grown horse's brain is about the size of a human child's brain.

127. **True.** Horses like sweets but will reject sour or bitter flavors.

128. **True.** A horse heart weighs eight to ten pounds, and a human heart is usually less than one pound.

129. **False.** Horses can get sunburned, especially on pink-skinned areas.

130. **True.** If a horse's ears are cold, then the horse is cold.

131. **False.** Horses drink around 10 gallons of water per day. They need more water in hotter weather or when they are highly active.

132. HORSES CAN ROTATE THEIR EARS IN A HALF CIRCLE (180 DEGREES).

TRUE OR FALSE?

133. HORSES CANNOT BREATHE THROUGH THEIR MOUTHS.

TRUE OR FALSE?

134. NEWBORN HORSES EAT GRASS.

TRUE OR FALSE?

135. HORSE HOOVES KEEP GROWING.

TRUE OR FALSE?

136. HORSES EAT MEAT.

TRUE OR FALSE?

137. A HORSE SHOULD ONLY CARRY ABOUT 10 PERCENT OF ITS OWN BODYWEIGHT.

TRUE OR FALSE?

132. **True.** Horses have 16 muscles in each of their ears and can move them to better take in the source of a sound.

133. **True.** Horses can only breathe through their nostrils and nasal passages.

134. **False.** Baby foals feed on their mothers' milk.

135. **True.** Horse hooves have to be trimmed (like fingernails) every 6 to 12 weeks.

136. **False.** Horses are herbivores and eat a fully plant-based diet.

137. **False.** Horses can safely carry about 20 percent of their bodyweight.

138. HORSES HAVE FOUR DIFFERENT GAITS, OR WAYS OF MOVING.

TRUE OR FALSE?

139. HORSES NEED A LOT OF SLEEP.

TRUE OR FALSE?

140. A "ZONKEY" IS CREATED WHEN A ZEBRA MATES WITH A DONKEY.

TRUE OR FALSE?

141. THE LARGEST BIRD EGG IS AN OSTRICH EGG.

TRUE OR FALSE?

142. BIRDS HAVE SMALL EYES.

TRUE OR FALSE?

143. OWLS CANNOT MOVE THEIR EYES.

TRUE OR FALSE?

See the back of the page to find out.

138. **True.** They can walk, trot, canter, and gallop.

 139. **False.** Horses' total sleep time averages only two to three hours per night in 15-minute increments.

140. **True.** Zonkeys cannot reproduce together, but mating a zebra with a donkey can result in the hybrid of the two species.

141. **True.** An ostrich egg is about the size of a cantaloupe.

 142. **False.** Birds' eyes take up almost half of their heads. In many birds, a large part of the eye cannot be seen because they are covered by skin and feathers.

143. **True.** To see in different directions, owls rotate their heads instead of moving their eyes.

144. A single chicken can lay 250 eggs each year.

TRUE OR FALSE?

145. Male birds are usually more colorful than female birds.

TRUE OR FALSE?

146. Kiwi birds have excellent eyesight.

TRUE OR FALSE?

147. Chickens that lay brown eggs usually have brown or red earlobes.

TRUE OR FALSE?

See the back of the page to find out.

144. **True.** Chickens usually begin laying eggs at around six months old. The number of eggs they produce tends to decrease with age.

145. **True.** Male birds' more colorful plumage is used to attract female birds and to warn other male birds away from their territory.

146. **False.** Kiwi birds have the smallest eyes and visual fields of any birds, and many fully sightless kiwi have been observed in nature. They rely on other senses to find food.

147. **True.** Chicken egg colors usually can be predicted by their ear color, but there are some exceptions.

148. THE ONLY ORGANS INVOLVED IN A BIRD'S SINGING ARE THE LUNGS.

TRUE OR FALSE?

149. WOODPECKERS CAN SING.

TRUE OR FALSE?

150. WOODPECKERS EAT ANTS.

TRUE OR FALSE?

See the back of the page to find out.

148. **False.** Birds have a specialized organ known as the syrinx that enables their singing. Some songbirds can even control each half of their syrinx separately to sing with two different voices at the same time.

149. **False.** They communicate by drumming their beaks on surfaces and can also chirp or chatter.

150. **True.** They can eat as many as 2,000 ants a day.

151. A bird can have thousands of feathers.

TRUE OR FALSE?

152. Flamingos bend their knees backwards.

TRUE OR FALSE?

153. A bird of prey can weigh 50 pounds.

TRUE OR FALSE?

154. The most common wild bird in the world is the sparrow.

TRUE OR FALSE?

155. Most wild birds live long lives.

TRUE OR FALSE?

See the back of the page to find out.

151. **True.** While a hummingbird can have fewer than 1,000 feathers, a whistling swan can have as many as 25,000 feathers.

 152. **False.** When a flamingo appears to be bending its leg, it is the ankle they are bending. The knee is usually hidden by feathers.

153. **False.** The heaviest bird of prey, the Andean Condor, weighs up to 33 pounds.

154. **False.** There are an estimated 1.5 billion red-billed quelea in the wild, mostly in Africa.

155. **False.** Most birds in the wild do not have long lives because of the number of threats to their safety, including predators, building strikes, habitat loss, and food scarcity.

156. SOME WILD BIRDS LIVE MORE THAN 50 YEARS.

TRUE OR FALSE?

157. PENGUINS ARE SLOW SWIMMERS.

TRUE OR FALSE?

158. SOME BIRDS CAN FLY AS HIGH ABOVE THE EARTH'S SURFACE AS JET AIRPLANES.

TRUE OR FALSE?

159. A EUROPEAN WREN CAN SING MORE THAN 700 DIFFERENT NOTES A MINUTE.

TRUE OR FALSE?

See the back of the page to find out.

156. **True.** The large wandering albatross may live over 80 years.

157. **False.** Some penguins can swim more than 20 miles per hour.

158. **True.** In 1973, a Griffon Vulture collided with an airplane at an altitude of 37,000 feet.

159. **True.** A European wren's song can be heard more than five football fields away.

160. THE FLIGHTLESS ELEPHANT BIRD WEIGHED ABOUT **1,000** POUNDS.

TRUE OR FALSE? 🐾 🐾 🐾 🐾

161. THE FASTEST FLYING BIRD IS THE BALD EAGLE.

TRUE OR FALSE? 🥚 🥚 🥚 🥚

162. OSTRICHES HAVE THREE TOES.

TRUE OR FALSE? 🐾 🐾 🐾 🐾

See the back of the page to find out.

160. **True.** The enormous elephant bird, native to Madagascar, became extinct some 500 years ago.

161. **False.** Eagles top out at 99 miles per hour when diving at prey. The Peregrine Falcon can reach speeds over 200 miles per hour when it enters a hunting dive.

 162. **False.** Ostriches only have two toes: one large toe and a smaller toe for balance.

163. BIRDS CAN FLY FOR MORE THAN A YEAR WITHOUT SETTLING ON WATER OR LAND.

TRUE OR FALSE?

164. BIRDS FLY IN FORMATION TO SAVE ENERGY.

TRUE OR FALSE?

165. BIRD POOP (KNOWN AS GUANO) WAS A HIGHLY SOUGHT COMMODITY IN THE 19TH CENTURY.

TRUE OR FALSE?

166. CROWS CAN RECOGNIZE HUMAN FACES.

TRUE OR FALSE?

167. A GROUP OF CROWS IS CALLED A MURDER.

TRUE OR FALSE?

163. **True.** The Sooty Tern is known to fly over the ocean for years at a time.

164. **True.** Birds flying in formation have less wind resistance. It's also easier to keep track of the whole flock.

165. **True.** Guano was considered very valuable as a soil fertilizer.

166. **True.** Crows particularly recognize human faces they associate with bad experiences.

167. **True.** A group of crows can also be called a congress.

168. A GROUP OF OWLS IS CALLED A SENATE.

TRUE OR FALSE? ← ← ← ←

169. A GROUP OF FLAMINGOS IS CALLED A BEVY.

TRUE OR FALSE?

170. BALD EAGLES MADE THE WORLD'S LARGEST BIRD'S NEST.

TRUE OR FALSE?

171. THE CASSOWARY IS A PEACEFUL BIRD.

TRUE OR FALSE?

172. THE SKULL OF SNAKES IS ONE BONE.

TRUE OR FALSE?

← 168. **False.** A group of owls can be called a parliament.

◄ 169. **False.** They are called a flamboyance. Bevy is usually used for quail.

🐾 170. **True.** According to Guinness World Records, a bald eagle nest found in Florida in 1963 was nearly 10 feet wide and weighed more than 4,000 pounds.

🦶 171. **False.** The cassowary has a reputation as the world's "most dangerous bird," and has been known to use its powerful kick to inflict injuries on people and other animals.

🐍 172. **False.** Snake skulls are made of small bones so they can open their mouths wide to eat large prey.

173. Chameleons change color to camouflage.

TRUE OR FALSE?

174. Reptiles are not slimy.

TRUE OR FALSE?

175. Some species of geckos shed their tails.

TRUE OR FALSE?

176. Rattlesnakes bear live young.

TRUE OR FALSE?

177. The two main parts of a turtle's shell are the "lid" and the "pot."

TRUE OR FALSE?

178. Snails don't sleep.

TRUE OR FALSE?

173. **False.** Chameleons are naturally camouflaged and change color mostly related to temperature changes and to communicate.

174. **True.** Reptiles do not have sweat glands to produce moisture. Their skin is usually cool and dry.

175. **True.** Geckos can drop their tails to escape predators. Most geckos' tails grow back.

176. **True.** Most snakes lay eggs but rattlesnakes, boa constrictors, and garter snakes are examples of snakes that bear live young.

177. **False.** The two main parts of a turtle's shell are the "carapace" (top) and the "plastron" (bottom).

178. **False.** Some snails can sleep for up to three years at a time.

179. AN OCTOPUS HAS FOUR HEARTS.

TRUE OR FALSE?

180. AN OCTOPUS HAS NINE BRAINS.

TRUE OR FALSE?

181. REINDEER CAN HAVE BLUE EYES.

TRUE OR FALSE?

182. SEA LIONS ARE GOOD DANCERS.

TRUE OR FALSE?

See the back of the page to find out.

179. **False.** Like most cephalopods, an octopus has three hearts.

180. **True.** A central brain controls the octopus's nervous system. There is also a smaller brain in each of its eight arms.

181. **True.** Reindeer eyes can turn blue in winter to help them see at lower light levels.

182. **True.** Sea lions are the first non-human mammal with a proven ability to keep a beat in time to music.

183. MOST BATS CAN'T WALK.

TRUE OR FALSE?

184. COWS CAN ONLY SLEEP LYING DOWN.

TRUE OR FALSE?

185. KOALA FINGERPRINTS ARE LIKE HUMAN FINGERPRINTS.

TRUE OR FALSE?

See the back of the page to find out.

183. **True.** The leg bones of most bats do not allow them to walk. Their bodies are specifically adapted to flying.

 184. **False.** Cows can only achieve REM (deep) sleep when they sleep lying down, but they can doze while standing.

185. **True.** Koala fingerprints have unique patterns and whorls similar to human fingerprints. Some criminal investigations in Australia have been hampered by koala fingerprints.

186. MALE LIONS DO MOST OF THE HUNTING.

TRUE OR FALSE?

187. BOTTLENOSE DOLPHINS ARE MOSTLY LEFT-HANDED.

TRUE OR FALSE?

188. FROGS CAN FREEZE WITHOUT DYING.

TRUE OR FALSE?

189. THE TOP SPEED OF AN OCTOPUS IS A SLOW SEVEN MILES PER HOUR.

TRUE OR FALSE?

190. ADULT SLOTH MOTHS ONLY LIVE ON SLOTHS.

TRUE OR FALSE?

191. FEMALE BATS GIVE BIRTH TO LARGE BABIES.

TRUE OR FALSE?

See the back of the page to find out.

186. **False.** Female lions do 90 percent of the hunting.

187. **False.** In 2019, research showed that 99 percent of the time, dolphins turn to their left, suggesting a right-handed bias.

188. **True.** Frogs can undergo repeated freeze-thaw cycles and still survive.

189. **False.** An octopus can move up to 25 miles per hour.

190. **True.** Sloth moths evolved to survive by eating algae on sloths' fur.

191. **True.** A baby bat can weigh up to a third its mother's weight at birth.

192. PAINTED TURTLES CAN BREATHE THROUGH THEIR BUTTS.

TRUE OR FALSE?

193. OTTERS HAVE THICK FUR.

TRUE OR FALSE?

194. ALLIGATORS REACH THEIR FULL SIZE BY THE AGE OF TWO.

TRUE OR FALSE?

195. SNOW LEOPARDS CAN MAKE A LOUD ROAR.

TRUE OR FALSE?

196. A GROUP OF RHINOS IS CALLED A CRASH.

TRUE OR FALSE?

192. **True.** A process called "cloacal respiration" enables painted turtles to get oxygen from water in winter.

193. **True.** Otters can have up to one million hairs per square inch.

194. **False.** Alligators often keep growing until they are around 25 to 30 years old.

195. **False.** Snow leopards have less developed vocal chords than other large cats and can purr, hiss, and growl. But they cannot roar.

196. **True.** Within the crash, male rhinos are called bulls and female rhinos are called cows.

197. GIANT ANTEATERS CAN HAVE TWO-FOOT-LONG TONGUES.

TRUE OR FALSE?

198. RATS CAN LAUGH.

TRUE OR FALSE?

199. WOMBAT POOP IS CYLINDRICAL.

TRUE OR FALSE?

200. SCORPIONS STARVE IF THEY DON'T EAT EVERY DAY.

TRUE OR FALSE?

197. **True.** Giant anteaters have the longest tongues of any mammal.

198. **True.** Rats have been observed making a laugh-like sound when tickled.

199. **False.** Wombat poop is cube shaped, which makes it easy for them to spot the territory of other wombats.

200. **False.** Scorpions can slow their metabolism when food is hard to find. Some species have been known to survive on one insect for a whole year.

201. ANTS DON'T HAVE LUNGS.

TRUE OR FALSE?

202. AN ANTEATER HAS A BIG MOUTH, FULL OF TEETH.

TRUE OR FALSE?

203. BUTTERFLIES CAN BE POISONOUS.

TRUE OR FALSE?

204. HIPPOS CAN'T RUN.

TRUE OR FALSE?

201. **True.** Ants breathe through tiny holes in their sides called spiracles.

202. **False.** A six-foot-long anteater's mouth is usually only an inch wide and is toothless and tube shaped.

203. **True.** African giant swallowtails have enough poisonous toxin to kill six cats.

204. **False.** Hippos can run faster than humans—up to 30 miles per hour.

205. SOME KANGAROOS CAN LIVE IN TREES.

TRUE OR FALSE?

206. A FLEA CAN JUMP 200 TIMES ITS OWN SIZE.

TRUE OR FALSE?

207. GARDEN CATERPILLARS HAVE MUSCLES IN THEIR HEADS.

TRUE OR FALSE?

See the back of the page to find out.

205. **True.** Tree kangaroos have tails that are longer than their head and body combined to make it easier to balance in trees.

206. **True.** Since a flea is only a few millimeters long, its jumping height of 10 inches (25 centimeters) is similar to a man jumping over a skyscraper.

207. **True.** They have 248 muscles in their heads.

208. COWS ONLY POOP ONCE A WEEK.

TRUE OR FALSE?

209. BLUE WHALE HEARTS BEAT FASTER THAN A HUMAN HEART.

TRUE OR FALSE?

210. A RHINOCEROS HORN IS MADE OUT OF IVORY.

TRUE OR FALSE?

211. GIRAFFES CAN SING.

TRUE OR FALSE?

212. DONKEYS HAVE AN EXTREMELY WIDE FIELD OF VISION.

TRUE OR FALSE?

See the back of the page to find out.

208. **False.** In a single day, a cow can poop 15 times.

209. **False.** Stanford University researchers found in 2019 that a blue whale's heart was beating a maximum of just 35 times a minute as it surfaced for air in the wild. The whale's rhythm slowed to only four beats per minute during other activities.

210. **False.** A rhinoceros horn is made of keratin, a protein also found in human fingernails and hair.

211. **False.** Giraffes don't sing and were thought to be nearly silent until as recently as 2015, when scientist found they hummed at a very low-frequency most humans can't hear.

212. **True.** The placement of a donkey's eyes enables them to see all four of their feet at the same time.

213. ONLY HALF OF A DOLPHIN'S BRAIN SLEEPS AT A TIME.

TRUE OR FALSE?

214. HIPPOPOTAMUSES ARE MOSTLY SILENT.

TRUE OR FALSE?

ugh!

213. **True.** The other non-sleeping half enables the dolphin to surface for air and to stay alert against predators and other threats.

214. **False.** Hippos are thought to be one of Africa's loudest animals. Some hippo vocalizations have been measured at 115 decibels—almost as loud as a jet plane during takeoff.

215. HIPPOS CAN'T FLOAT.

TRUE OR FALSE?

216. HIPPO SWEAT IS BLACK.

TRUE OR FALSE?

217. STARFISH HAVE FIVE EYES.

TRUE OR FALSE?

218. GIRAFFE HEARTS PUMP TWICE AS HARD AS COW HEARTS.

TRUE OR FALSE?

219. BUTTERFLIES HAVE SKELETONS ON THE OUTSIDE OF THEIR BODIES.

TRUE OR FALSE?

215. **True.** Hippos spend a lot of time in water, but they are too dense to float or swim. They mostly move around in water by pushing themselves off the bottom or walking on the riverbed surface.

216. **False.** Hippo sweat is pink or red.

217. **True.** Starfish have one eye at the end of each leg.

218. **True.** A giraffe heart pumps very hard to get blood up its long neck to its brain.

219. **True.** Like most insects, butterflies have an exoskeleton.

220. GIANT SQUID HAVE RELATIVELY SMALL EYES.

TRUE OR FALSE?   ← ← ← ←

221. THE COLOR RED MAKES BULLS ANGRY.

TRUE OR FALSE?

222. MALE BALD EAGLES ARE LARGER THAN THE FEMALES.

TRUE OR FALSE?

223. AFRICAN ELEPHANTS HAVE 32 TEETH TO CHEW THEIR FOOD.

TRUE OR FALSE?

224. MOOSE HAVE POOR VISION.

TRUE OR FALSE?

See the back of the page to find out.

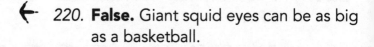

220. **False.** Giant squid eyes can be as big as a basketball.

221. **False.** Bulls are partially colorblind.

222. **False.** Female bald eagles are up to one-third larger than males.

223. **False.** Elephants have only four molar-like teeth to chew their food.

224. **True.** Moose have an excellent sense of hearing and smell to make up for their poor eyesight.

225. SOME MAMMALS LAY EGGS.

TRUE OR FALSE?

226. KINKAJOUS CAN ROTATE THEIR FEET.

TRUE OR FALSE?

227. FLAMINGOS ARE BORN PINK.

TRUE OR FALSE?

228. AN OTTER'S POOP CAN SMELL LIKE VIOLETS.

TRUE OR FALSE?

See the back of the page to find out.

225. **True.** The echidna and platypus are egg-laying mammals.

226. **True.** Kinkajous rotate their feet so that can run equally fast in any direction.

227. **False.** Flamingos turn pink from eating algae, larvae, and shrimp rich in beta-carotene, but they are a dull gray-white when first born.

228. **True.** Otter poop is called "spraint" and gives off a floral odor.

229. SNAKES CAN'T FLY.

   TRUE OR FALSE?

230. MANATEES FART TO REGULATE THEIR BUOYANCY.

   TRUE OR FALSE?

DIVE! DIVE!

231. SAND TIGER SHARKS EAT THEIR SMALLER SIBLINGS BEFORE EVEN BEING BORN.

   TRUE OR FALSE?

See the back of the page to find out.

229. **False.** Flying tree snakes can glide as far as 300 feet.

230. **True.** Manatees can hold in farts to float and release farts to sink.

231. **True.** While gestating in their mother's womb, sand tiger shark embryos eat each other until only one is left in each of the mother's two uterine horns.

232. SPIDERS CAN'T FLY.

TRUE OR FALSE?

233. CLOWNFISH ARE ALL BORN FEMALE.

TRUE OR FALSE?

234. NO ANIMAL CAN SURVIVE IN SPACE.

TRUE OR FALSE?

235. THE FEMALE KOMODO DRAGON CAN REPRODUCE WITHOUT MATING.

TRUE OR FALSE?

236. HIPPO TEETH CAN BE 20 INCHES LONG.

TRUE OR FALSE?

232. **False.** While spiders don't have wings, multiple spider species can use a process called "ballooning"—releasing threads of silk that catch air currents—to fly.

 233. **False.** Clownfish are all born male and can change their sex to become the dominant female.

 234. **False.** Microscopic water bears, also known as tardigrades, have been shown in experiments to be able to withstand the harsh environmental conditions of space.

235. **True.** Female Komodo dragons can lay eggs on their own when kept away from male Komodo dragons.

236. **True.** The hippo has long been thought to be one of the most dangerous land mammals, but its teeth are mostly used in defense or in fighting against other hippos.

237. SNOW LEOPARDS ARE AGGRESSIVE TOWARDS PEOPLE.

TRUE OR FALSE?

238. MARINE IGUANAS SNEEZE FREQUENTLY.

TRUE OR FALSE?

239. AFRICAN ELEPHANTS HAVE EARS SHAPED LIKE THE CONTINENT OF AFRICA.

TRUE OR FALSE?

240. GIANT PANDAS ARE DEAF.

TRUE OR FALSE?

241. SNOW LEOPARDS OFTEN SLEEP WITH THEIR TAILS COVERING THEIR FACES.

TRUE OR FALSE?

242. FOR SHORT DISTANCES, GRIZZLY BEARS CAN RUN FASTER THAN HORSES.

TRUE OR FALSE?

237. **False.** Unlike other big cats, there has never been a verified snow leopard attack on humans.

238. **True.** Sneezing expels excess salt from the glands near a marine iguana's nose.

239. **True.** Asian elephants have smaller, rounder ears than African elephants.

240. **False.** Pandas have excellent hearing and can even hear ultrasonic sounds.

241. **True.** Snow leopards wrap their tails around themselves for extra warmth.

242. **True.** Grizzly bears can run up to 35 mile per hour.

243. TURKEYS CAN'T FLY.

TRUE OR FALSE?

244. SKUNKS HAVE A POOR SENSE OF SMELL.

TRUE OR FALSE?

245. TIGERS CAN SWIM.

TRUE OR FALSE?

246. GIRAFFES AND HUMANS HAVE THE SAME NUMBER OF BONES IN THEIR NECKS.

TRUE OR FALSE?

Answers for previous page.

243. **False.** Wild turkeys can fly up to 55 miles per hour.

244. **False.** They have an excellent sense of smell and hearing but have poor vision.

245. **True.** Unlike some kinds of cats, tigers are strong swimmers and deliberately bathe in ponds, lakes, and rivers to keep cool.

246. **True.** Giraffes and humans both have seven neck bones but the giraffe bones are much bigger.

247. VAMPIRE BAT BITES ARE PAINFUL.

TRUE OR FALSE?

248. PREGNANT NINE-BANDED ARMADILLOS ALWAYS GIVE BIRTH TO FOUR BABIES.

TRUE OR FALSE?

249. A TORTOISE CAN WEIGH AS MUCH AS A BROWN BEAR.

TRUE OR FALSE?

250. EMPEROR PENGUINS CAN SWIM AND DIVE TO 1,500 FEET DEPTHS.

TRUE OR FALSE?

251. KIWI BIRDS EAT DURING THE DAY.

TRUE OR FALSE?

252. ALPACAS ROAM WILD IN MOUNTAINOUS REGIONS.

TRUE OR FALSE?

247. **False.** The teeth of vampire bats are so sharp, their prey might not feel the bite at all.

248. **True.** Nine-banded armadillos nearly always give birth to identical quadruplets.

249. **True.** A male giant tortoise can weigh over 500 pounds.

250. **True.** Emperor penguins can naturally dive deep and can stay underwater without surfacing for nearly half an hour.

251. **False.** They forage at night and have nostrils at the end of their long beaks.

252. **False.** There are no known wild alpacas. Alpacas are mostly raised for their fine wool.

253. BEETLES MAKE UP ABOUT 40 PERCENT OF ALL INSECT SPECIES.

TRUE OR FALSE?

254. SPIDERS ARE INSECTS.

TRUE OR FALSE?

255. THERE ARE MORE THAN A MILLION ANTS FOR EVERY HUMAN BEING IN THE WORLD.

TRUE OR FALSE?

256. THERE ARE VERY FEW INSECTS IN ANTARCTICA.

TRUE OR FALSE?

257. INSECTS HAVE EIGHT LEGS.

TRUE OR FALSE?

258. INSECTS BREATHE THROUGH THEIR MOUTHS.

TRUE OR FALSE?

See the back of the page to find out.   111

253. **True.** There are more than 380,000 species of beetles.

254. **False.** Spiders are arachnids with two body parts. Insects have three body parts.

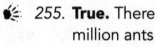 255. **True.** There are approximately 1.3 million ants for each of the 7.7 billion people in the world.

256. **True.** Antarctica only has one native species of insect, a wingless midge.

257. **False.** Insects have six legs.

258. **False.** Insects breathe through their sides.

259. INSECTS DON'T HAVE BLOOD VESSELS.

TRUE OR FALSE? ← ← ← ←

260. INSECT BLOOD IS RED.

TRUE OR FALSE?

261. INSECTS EXISTED BEFORE THE DINOSAURS.

TRUE OR FALSE?

262. DRAGONFLIES HAVE MORE THAN 30,000 PIECES IN THEIR EYES.

TRUE OR FALSE?

263. A MALE HORSEFLY CAN FLY FASTER THAN THE HIGHWAY SPEED LIMIT FOR CARS.

TRUE OR FALSE?

← 259. **True.** Insects have an open circulatory system so their blood is not contained within blood vessels.

🖐 260. **False.** Insect "blood" is called hemolymph and it is typically clear. It can also be green or yellow.

🐾 261. **True.** Insects were around 200 million years before dinosaurs.

262. **True.** Dragonflies have compound eyes consisting of pixel-like facets, or ommatidia, that create a mosaic image.

263. **True.** A male horsefly can fly up to 90 miles per hour.

264. A TERMITE CAN LAY AN EGG EVERY TWO OR THREE SECONDS.

TRUE OR FALSE?

265. INSECTS DON'T HAVE EARS.

TRUE OR FALSE?

266. ALL CATERPILLARS HAVE NO MORE THAN FOUR EYES.

TRUE OR FALSE?

267. NO INSECTS CAN BREATHE UNDERWATER.

TRUE OR FALSE?

264. **True.** A termite queen can lay more than 30,000 eggs in a single day.

265. **False.** Insects can have ears on their forelegs, wings, antennae, and other places on their bodies, yet rarely on their heads.

266. **False.** Most caterpillars have 12 eyes.

267. **False.** The water scorpion can breathe from underwater using its snorkel-like "tail."

268. A HORNET'S FAVORITE FOOD IS HONEY.

TRUE OR FALSE?

269. HOUSEFLIES FIND FOOD WITH THEIR FEET.

TRUE OR FALSE?

See the back of the page to find out.

268. **False.** A hornet's favorite food is a honeybee.

 269. **True.** Houseflies taste with their feet and palps before eating through their proboscis.

270. INSECTS PRODUCE "ANTIFREEZE."

TRUE OR FALSE?

271. SILK MOTHS CAN'T SMELL.

TRUE OR FALSE?

272. TRUE FLIES HAVE TWO PAIRS OF WINGS.

TRUE OR FALSE?

273. SOME SPIDERS CAN WALK ON WATER.

TRUE OR FALSE?

274. A FISH CAN HAVE TWO EYES ON THE SAME SIDE OF ITS BODY.

TRUE OR FALSE?

275. ALL SPIDERS MAKE WEBS.

TRUE OR FALSE?

270. **True.** Some insects survive cold weather by producing their own kind of "antifreeze" proteins.

271. **False.** Silk moths have a very fine sense of smell. Male silk moths can detect just few hundred molecules of female chemicals among 25 quintillion molecules in a cubic centimeter of air.

272. **False.** Flies have one pair of wings and sometimes none at all. They may also have a hind pair of "wings" called halteres simply for balance.

273. **True.** Water spiders can walk on water.

274. **True.** Mature flat fish like flounder and halibut can have two eyes on the same side.

275. **False.** Some spiders hunt their prey rather than using webs to trap prey.

276. SPIDERS ENTER HOUSES BY CLIMBING UP DRAINS IN SINKS AND SHOWERS.

TRUE OR FALSE?

277. THE SILK STRANDS IN A SPIDER WEB ARE VERY WEAK.

TRUE OR FALSE?

278. MANY SPIDERS HAVE SHORT HAIRS ON THEIR FEET.

TRUE OR FALSE?

279. SPIDERS CHEW AND SWALLOW SOLID PIECES OF THEIR PREY.

TRUE OR FALSE?

280. ANTS ARE VERY STRONG.

TRUE OR FALSE?

281. CRICKETS CAN HELP YOU ESTIMATE THE TEMPERATURE.

TRUE OR FALSE?

See the back of the page to find out.

276. **False.** Most modern drains contain a liquid-filled sediment trap that spiders can't get through.

277. **False.** The strands of silk in a spider web are five times stronger than a piece of steel the same size.

278. **True.** The short hairs enable a spider to walk on vertical surfaces or even upside down on a ceiling.

279. **False.** Spiders apply digestive juices to their prey to start dissolving it, then suck up the fluid.

280. **True.** They can carry up to 100 times their body weight.

281. **True.** Count the number of cricket chirps in 15 seconds, then add 37. That total is an estimate of the temperature (in degrees Fahrenheit).

282. Termites eat faster when rock music is playing.

TRUE OR FALSE?

283. Giraffes give birth standing up.

TRUE OR FALSE?

284. Lions purr.

TRUE OR FALSE?

He LIKES you!

See the back of the page to find out.

282. **True.** Studies done on termites show they chew through wood faster when rock music is playing. Scientists believe this is because the music vibrates the wood at a frequency that termites find appealing.

283. **True.** The baby giraffe drops 5 to 6 feet to the ground and is able to stand up, walk, and even run soon after birth.

284. **False.** Unlike smaller cats, lions can roar but not purr.

285. Baby elephants often suck their trunks.

TRUE OR FALSE? ← ← ← ←

286. Pangolins have short tongues.

TRUE OR FALSE?

287. Bonobos can be bald.

TRUE OR FALSE?

288. Bonobos are vegetarians.

TRUE OR FALSE?

289. The dromedary camel is extinct in the wild.

TRUE OR FALSE?

290. All camels have two humps.

TRUE OR FALSE?

See the back of the page to find out.

285. **True.** Baby elephants suck on their trunks much like human babies suck their thumbs.

286. **False.** Pangolins (sometimes known as scaly anteaters) can have tongues longer than their head and body combined.

287. **True.** In the wild, most bonobos have full heads of hair, but in captivity, they are often bald due to excessive mutual grooming.

288. **False.** Bonobos eat fruit and plants as well as small animals and fish.

289. **True.** The dromedary camel has been extinct in its native habitat, but a feral population still lives in Australia.

290. **False.** The Bactrian camel has two humps but the dromedary camel has one hump.

291. THE CAPE BUFFALO IS A GRASS EATER.

TRUE OR FALSE?

292. GORILLAS ARE THE LARGEST OF THE GREAT APES.

TRUE OR FALSE?

293. GORILLAS HAVE BIG APPETITES.

TRUE OR FALSE?

294. APES HAVE TAILS.

TRUE OR FALSE?

295. ALL RHINOCEROSES LIVE IN AFRICA.

TRUE OR FALSE?

296. RHINOCEROSES RARELY ATTACK HUMANS.

TRUE OR FALSE?

See the back of the page to find out.

291. **True.** The Cape buffalo is a grass eater but it is still widely considered dangerous to people due to its history of goring attacks.

292. **True.** Eastern lowland gorillas are the largest of the living great apes.

293. **True.** Gorillas consume up to 40 pounds of vegetation a day.

294. **False.** Most monkeys have tails. Apes do not.

295. **False.** Two species of rhinoceros live in Africa and three species live in Asia.

296. **True.** Rhinoceros attacks on humans are extremely rare.

297. THE WILDEBEEST IS ALSO CALLED THE GNU.

   TRUE OR FALSE?

298. WILDEBEESTS ARE LONERS.

   TRUE OR FALSE?

299. BOTH MALE AND FEMALE WILDEBEESTS HAVE HORNS.

   TRUE OR FALSE?

300. MONGOOSE CAN HUNT DEADLY COBRAS.

   TRUE OR FALSE?

Didn't feel a thing.

unk!

See the back of the page to find out.

297. **True.** Wildebeest is the name in Afrikaans, meaning "wild beast" or "wild cattle."

 298. **False.** Wildebeests live in large herds, sometimes mixed with zebras.

299. **True.** The male wildebeest horns are typically larger and thicker than female horns.

300. **True.** Mongooses are largely resistant to the venom of scorpions and snakes.

301. WOLF HOWLS CAN BE HEARD UP TO 10 MILES AWAY.

TRUE OR FALSE?

302. CHEETAHS HUNT ONLY AT NIGHT.

TRUE OR FALSE?

303. HONEY BADGERS ARE RESISTANT TO BEE STINGS.

TRUE OR FALSE?

304. A FULLY GROWN MOUSE LEMUR WEIGHS AN AVERAGE OF ONE POUND.

TRUE OR FALSE?

See the back of the page to find out.

301. **True.** On the Arctic tundra, wolf howls travel great distances of as much as 10 miles.

302. **False.** Cheetahs mostly hunt alone, but they hunt in the daytime, usually in the morning or before dusk.

303. **True.** Honey badgers' skin is so thick that attacks like bee stings cannot penetrate it.

304. **False.** While the indri lemur can weigh up to 20 pounds, the mouse lemur is tiny and weighs about one ounce.

AVAILABLE NOW!